I0465653

FOREX GUIDE FOR FOREX TRADERS

BY
A. W. ANTONIO

Table of Contents

CHAPTER ONE

FOREX ACCOUNT TYPES

Forex trading has gradually gained massive attention than one would have imagined about a decade ago. Given its technicalities and risks involved, one would have thought that only a few people would summon enough impetus to plunge the seemingly complex forex market. Its reality has however proven to the contrary, that in spite of the difficulties and complexities inherent in the forex market, people are still navigating the market by the day. Not just that, but also making some good fortunes for themselves from this.

Beyond reasonable doubts, we can agree that forex trading is one of the most popular ways to invest and make money online in this era. One crucial factor to consider in forex trading is choosing the right forex account type. This section is particularly intended to explore various forex account types and further help you understand the differences between them. This will guide you through making a selection of any one of them.

Some of the most common forex account types are presented below in no particular order:

- Demo account
- Standard Account
- Micro Account
- Managed Account
- Islamic Account

DEMO ACCOUNT

A demo forex account is a simulated trading account that is offered by brokers that allow traders to practice forex trading in a risk-free environment. It is also referred to as a practice account and is mostly used for learning how to trade the forex market without being exposed to real time risks associated with the market. A demo account is quite identical to the standard forex account and mimics real market conditions using virtual currency, enabling traders to experience trading strategies, market dynamics and platform features without necessarily being exposed to financial risks in real time. Some of the benefits of using a demo forex account type include the following:

i. It helps traders gain proficiency in using features and tools in the trading platform, thereby making their transition to a live account smoother and more efficient.

ii. It offers traders practical experience in executing trades, analyzing charts and using trading tools.

iii. The absence of financial risk offers traders trading experience without the psychological stress associated with real time trading.

iv. Some demo accounts offer traders detailed reports and analytics to help them evaluate their trading performances.

STANDARD ACCOUNT

The standard forex account type is the most common type of forex account offered by forex brokers to traders. They provide standard trading conditions with typical contract sizes and leverage. Standard accounts are designed for traders with a good understanding of the forex market and allows traders to trade standard lots of currency pairs. Each standard lot in a standard account represents 100,000 units of the base currency, and makes it suitable for the more experienced traders seeking greater exposure and returns. Below are some of the benefits of the standard forex account type:

i. Standard accounts mostly offer traders advanced trading features and tools which include technical indicators, sophisticated charting packages and automated trading options which further enhance the ability of the traders to analyze and execute trades.

ii. Standard accounts also offer traders the availability of higher leverage which allows them to control larger positions with relatively smaller amounts of capital.

iii. Due to higher contract sizes, standard accounts offers traders the potential of making higher profits for each trade, particularly those with strong understanding of movements in the market.

iv. Due to larger trade sizes and increased market activities, standard accounts offer better liquidity, which can further lead to a more efficient execution.

MICRO ACCOUNT

Micro forex accounts are particularly ideal for traders who want to trade with a very small amount of capital and also have more control over their risk management. In a micro account, each micro lot represents 1000 units of the base currency and also comes with lower minimum deposit requirements which also make it an ideal choice for beginners. The benefits of the micro account include the following:

i. Micro accounts typically require a smaller initial deposit compared to the standard account. This makes it easier for new traders to start trading without very substantial capital.

ii. The use of micro lots helps in limiting potential losses and managing risks more efficiently.

iii. Many brokers offer lower spreads and commissions on micro accounts, making it more cost effective to trade smaller positions.

MANAGED ACCOUNT

For a managed forex account type, a professional money manager trades and manages the account on behalf of a client. In this case, the account is funded by the investor and trading decisions are transferred to and handled by a professional trader on behalf of the investor. Put differently, for a managed account, the investor delegates discretionary authority to the manager to make trading decisions, execute trades and manage the account's portfolio based on mutually agreed strategies and objectives by the investor and the account manager. Below are some of the benefits of a managed account:

i. Managed accounts are overseen by experienced professionals who have deep understanding of the forex market, and whose expertise can yield better trading outcomes for their clients.

ii. Experienced account managers employ various risk management strategies to prevent the impact of significant losses on the investment.

iii. Managed accounts have the potential of achieving higher returns compared to some self managed accounts.

ISLAMIC ACCOUNT

The Islamic forex account type is also known as a swap-free account. It is sharia-compliant as it is designed to adhere to the principles of Islamic finance. Consequently, this type of account prohibits certain financial activities including earning or paying interests, and also engaging in speculative trading practices that are deemed excessive. Islamic accounts ensure that their users participate in the forex market in a manner consistent with the Islamic religious beliefs. Some of the benefits of the Islamic account are as follows:

i. Islamic forex accounts prohibit swap fees thereby making the cost of holding a position transparent and also consistent with sharia laws.

ii. With Islamic accounts, there is provision of a clear structure for fees and trading costs, which reduces the potential for hidden charges or excessive speculation.

iii. These accounts align with Islamic principles of ethical trading which fosters fair and transparent business practices.

CHOOSING A FOREX ACCOUNT TYPE

Just as there are different types of forex traders, so are there different forex account types that suit the expectations and needs of the traders. From beginners, to market experts, to investors who need fund managers, there are various accounts designed to meet individual specifications and needs. Choosing the right forex account type is essential for trading success in the trading market. It is advisable for traders to choose a forex account type which is suitable to their individual needs, and based on their level of experience in the forex market.

CHAPTER TWO

RISK MANAGEMENT IN TRADING

Risks! Is there any human endeavor that is devoid of risks? Can one really live life without any form of risk whatsoever? Someone once noted that life is so risky that you probably won't get out of it alive. For some people, this statement alone can scare life out of them, but scary as the statement may sound, it sends a very critical message on how risky life generally can be. Even trading, just as any other human endeavors involves exposures to certain degrees of risks, especially given the high rates of volatilities and currency fluctuations that characterizes the forex market. These risks may not be completely avoided, but ignoring them is even worse.

Risk management in trading therefore becomes the most viable option when dealing with risks in trading.

WHAT IS RISK MANAGEMENT IN TRADING?

Risk management is inarguably a fundamental concept, especially in trading. Risk management in trading refers to the process of analyzing, evaluating and addressing potential risks that are related with financial transactions so as to minimize losses and optimize returns. It involves effective strategies aimed at identifying, assessing and mitigating potential risks involved in trading in order to protect capital and also achieve long term success in forex trading. It is quite a proactive approach that aims to control uncertainties and volatilities that are associated with trading activities.

It is important to understand that risk management in trading isn't merely a defensive strategy to shield against attacks inherent in the forex market, it is actually the very bedrock and cornerstone upon which successful trading activities are built. Risk management in trading therefore involves intelligent implementation of strategies and techniques to protect investments from unfavourable movements and unexpected events in the market. Effectively managing risks in trading actually requires some level of knowledge and skill because it involves the ability to make informed decisions and take appropriate actions towards minimizing and controlling identified risks. These risks may come from different sources including economic shifts, fluctuations and market volatility, unforeseen market dynamics and even geopolitical events that may have impacts on market performance and operations.

KEY COMPONENTS OF RISK MANAGEMENT IN TRADING

There are various components of risk management in trading which are crucial and ought to be given consideration when creating a framework for risk management in trading. Some of the key components of risk management in trading includes, but are not limited to the following:

- Risk identification
- Risk assessment
- Risk mitigation
- Risk monitoring

RISK IDENTIFICATION

This is pretty much the first step in risk management because before a thing can be managed, it must first be identified. Put differently, a risk that has not been identified cannot be properly managed. You have to be able to identify it in order to be able to manage it. So, the first thing is to identify potential risks that could impact trading positions. This may include market risks, operational risks, or even systematic risks that may arise from various sources. Haven identified a range or list of potential risks, the risks can be ranked or categorized into low, medium and high risks. This will further inform the decision on which risk(s) to attend to, and in what order.

RISK ASSESSMENT

Haven scaled through the first phase of identifying potential risks, the next phase involved in the components of risk management in trading is risk assessment. Once risks have been identified, traders would need to assess the likelihood or chances of being affected by the identified risks, and also the potential impact of such risks on their trading activities. Risk assessment may sometimes involve quantifying risks in order to better understand their implications on portfolio performance and trading positions.

RISK MITIGATION

One of the core objectives of risk management in trading is to protect capital and reduce the trader's level of exposure to trading risks generally. This can be achievable through risk mitigation strategy. So, after a potential risk has been assessed to understand its potential impact level, a wise trader is expected to develop and also implement effective strategies that can effectively mitigate the risk. In some cases, these strategies may involve setting stop-loss orders, diversifying investments, application of hedging techniques, and also employing proper position sizing among other options.

RISK MONITORING

Risk management in trading would require a substantial level of continuous risk monitoring which is essential for the purpose of tracking changes in market conditions, especially given the dynamic nature of the trading market. Risk monitoring is very crucial especially for assessing the effectiveness of risk management strategies, so as to be able to determine required action points and decisions to make. Risk monitoring would require traders to stay vigilant and also make adjustments in their risk management approach in order to adapt to evolving market dynamics.

HOW TO APPLY RISK MANAGEMENT IN TRADING

Applying risk management in trading is crucial for protecting trading capital and for maximizing the potentials for long term success. Below are some of the recommended ways to apply risk management in trading: Set Risk Tolerance: you should be able to determine the maximum amount of capital you are willing to risk in any given trade. This should be a small fraction of your total trading capital.

Use Stop-Loss Orders: it is advisable to use stop-loss orders to limit potential losses in a given trade. The stop-loss level can be set based on risk tolerance as well as market conditions.

Diversification: risks can be spread by trading different assets or even different markets. It is not advisable to put all of one's capital into one trade or asset class.

Risk-Reward Ratio: for each trade, it is wise to evaluate the potential reward relative to the risk associated. Always aim for a favorable risk-reward ratio to ensure that the potential losses do not outweigh the potential profits.

Position Sizing: you should calculate the position size for each trade based on your risk tolerance and also the distance to your stop-loss level. Your position size should be adjusted accordingly to ensure that you are not risking more than you can afford to lose.

Monitor and Adjust: regularly review your risk management strategies and make adjustments on them based on your trading performance and market conditions.

CHAPTER THREE

RECOMMENDED LOT SIZE FOR FOREX TRADING

One of the most critical decisions traders face is determining the correct lot size for forex trading. Choosing the appropriate lot size is essential because it directly impacts your risk management, capital allocation, and potential profits or losses. In this section, we will consider the factors influencing lot size selection and provide a detailed guide on the recommended lot size for your forex trading needs.

WHAT IS A LOT SIZE IN FOREX TRADING?

It is important to understand what lot size means in forex trading. Forex trades are conducted in standardized units called lots. The lot size refers to the number of currency units involved in a trade. In the forex market, there are three primary types of lot sizes:

Standard Lot: A standard lot is 100,000 units of the base currency in a forex trade. For example, if you are trading the EUR/USD currency pair, one standard lot equals 100,000 euros.

Mini Lot: A mini lot is 10,000 units of the base currency. This is one-tenth the size of a standard lot. For example, trading one mini lot of the EUR/USD pair would involve 10,000 euros.

Micro Lot: A micro lot is 1,000 units of the base currency, which is one-tenth of a mini lot and one-hundredth of a standard lot. For instance, trading one micro lot of the EUR/USD currency pair means you are trading 1,000 euros.

The lot size you choose determines the amount of money you control in the market, as well as your exposure to price fluctuations. Consequently, selecting the right lot size is crucial for effective risk management.

FACTORS TO CONSIDER WHEN SELECTING LOT SIZE FOR FOREX TRADING

When selecting the optimal lot size for forex trading, several factors must be considered. These factors include:

1. Account Size
2. Risk Tolerance
3. Leverage
4. Currency Pair Volatility
5. Trading Strategy
6. Risk Management Approach

ACCOUNT SIZE

Your account size or the amount of capital you have available for trading plays a significant role in determining the appropriate lot size. Larger account sizes can accommodate larger lot sizes without taking on excessive risk, while smaller accounts require more conservative lot sizing. The recommended lot size based on account size is as follows:

For small accounts (Below $1,000), Micro lots (1,000 units) or nano lots (100 units) are the recommended lot sizes.

For medium Accounts ($1,000 to $10,000), mini lots (10,000 units) is the recommended lot size.

For large Accounts (Above $10,000), standard lots (100,000 units) is the recommended lot size.

RISK TOLERANCE

Risk tolerance is the amount of risk a trader is willing to take on a trade. It varies from trader to trader and is influenced by factors such as financial goals, experience level, and psychological resilience. Generally, more risk-tolerant traders are comfortable with larger lot sizes, while risk-averse traders prefer smaller lot sizes to limit potential losses.

A widely accepted rule of thumb in forex trading is to risk no more than 1-2% of your total account balance on any single trade. To calculate the appropriate lot size based on your risk tolerance, follow these steps:

- Determine your risk per trade
- Calculate the pip value
- Set your stop-loss distance

LEVERAGE

Leverage allows traders to control larger positions with a smaller amount of capital. For example, with 100:1 leverage, a trader can control $100,000 worth of currency with just $1,000. While leverage can amplify profits, it can also magnify losses, making it essential to choose the right lot size based on your leverage ratio.

Traders with high leverage should be cautious when selecting lot sizes, as even small market movements can result in significant gains or losses. On the other hand, traders with low leverage can afford to take on slightly larger lot sizes, as their exposure to risk is lower.

CURRENCY PAIR VOLATILITY

Currency pair volatility refers to the amount of price movement a currency pair experiences over a given period. Some currency pairs are more volatile than others, meaning they experience larger price swings. Volatile currency pairs, such as GBP/JPY or EUR/AUD, can move hundreds of pips in a short period, increasing both the potential for profit and the risk of loss.

When trading volatile currency pairs, it's important to select a smaller lot size to reduce your risk exposure. Conversely, when trading less volatile pairs, such as EUR/USD or USD/CHF, traders can consider larger lot sizes, as price movements are generally more stable.

TRADING STRATEGY

The type of trading strategy you employ also plays a role in determining the appropriate lot size. Different strategies require different levels of risk exposure, trade duration, and capital allocation.

Scalping: Scalpers typically use standard or mini lots, but they must have strict risk controls, such as tight stop-loss orders, to avoid large losses.

Day Trading: Day traders can use mini or standard lots, depending on their risk tolerance and account size. However, they should ensure that they are not risking more than 1-2% of their account on any trade.

Swing Trading: Swing traders generally use micro or mini lots, as they need to manage risk over longer timeframes and larger price swings.

Position Trading: Position traders typically use micro lots or a combination of micro and mini lots to ensure that they are not overexposed to market fluctuations.

RISK MANAGEMENT APPROACH

Effective risk management is the cornerstone of successful forex trading, and your lot size should always align with your risk management strategy. By adhering to risk management principles, such as the 1-2% rule, you can prevent significant losses and preserve your trading capital. The recommended lot size based on risk management approach include:

Conservative Risk Management: Traders who follow conservative risk management practices should use micro or mini lots to minimize risk and avoid large drawdowns.

Aggressive Risk Management: Traders who take on more risk in pursuit of larger profits can consider using standard or mini lots, but they must have a solid plan for managing losses.

Choosing the correct lot size for forex trading is a critical decision that directly impacts your risk, profitability, and overall trading performance. By taking into account the factors highlighted in this section, traders can make informed decisions about the appropriate lot size for their trades.

Ultimately, successful forex trading is about managing risk while optimizing potential returns. By selecting the right lot size for your trading style and circumstances, you can enhance your chances of long-term success in the highly competitive forex market.

CHAPTER FOUR

HOW TO BECOME A SUCCESSFUL FOREX TRADER

To become a successful forex trader requires a blend of technical skills, analytical acumen, market knowledge, emotional discipline, and strategic planning. Forex trading is the largest financial market globally, with over $6 trillion traded daily.

Unlike other financial markets, the forex market operates 24/5, which provides an accessible trading environment. However, success in forex trading doesn't come by chance. It requires a methodical approach, continuous learning, and the right mindset. In this section, we will explore the essential steps and strategies necessary for becoming a successful forex trader.

UNDERSTANDING THE FOREX MARKET

To become a successful forex trader, you must have a good understanding of how the market works. The forex market operates differently from other financial markets such as stocks or commodities. Here are the key elements you need to understand:

CURRENCY PAIRS

Forex trading involves the buying and selling of currencies. Every transaction involves two currencies, referred to as a currency pair. The first currency is the base currency, and the second is the quote currency. For example, in the currency pair EUR/USD, EUR is the base currency and USD is the quote currency. Traders speculate on whether the base currency will strengthen or weaken against the quote currency.

MARKET PARTICIPANTS

The forex market includes a wide variety of participants; central banks, commercial banks, financial institutions, hedge funds, and individual traders like yourself. Understanding the influence of these participants, particularly central banks and financial institutions is critical, as they can significantly affect currency prices.

MARKET HOURS AND SESSIONS

The forex market operates in sessions based on global financial hubs: the London session, New York session, and Asian session. Understanding the peak times when the market is most liquid will allow you to make better trading decisions. For example, during the overlap between the London and New York sessions, liquidity and volatility are at their highest.

MASTERING FUNDAMENTAL AND TECHNICAL ANALYSIS

To become a successful forex trader, you need to know how to analyze the market. This is primarily done through two types of analysis: fundamental analysis and technical analysis.

FUNDAMENTAL ANALYSIS

Fundamental analysis in forex involves evaluating the macroeconomic factors that influence currency prices. These factors include:

Interest Rates: Central banks adjust interest rates to control inflation and stabilize their economies. Higher interest rates tend to strengthen a currency, while lower rates can weaken it.

Economic Indicators: Indicators such as GDP growth, inflation rates, unemployment data, and consumer spending give insight into a country's economic health. Strong economic performance generally leads to a stronger currency.

Geopolitical Events: Political instability, elections, trade agreements, and international conflicts can have significant impacts on currency values. Staying updated with global news is crucial for forex traders using fundamental analysis.

TECHNICAL ANALYSIS

Technical analysis involves studying past price movements to predict future trends. Forex traders often use charts, patterns, and technical indicators to find potential trading opportunities. The key tools used in technical analysis include:

Candlestick Patterns: Candlestick charts provide visual insights into market sentiment. Traders use these patterns (like the engulfing pattern, hammer, and shooting star) to predict price reversals or continuations.

Trend Lines: A trend line is drawn to connect the highs or lows of price movements. Identifying trends is one of the most fundamental aspects of forex trading.

Technical Indicators: Popular indicators include the Moving Average (MA), Relative Strength Index (RSI), Bollinger Bands, and Fibonacci Retracement Levels. These help traders gauge momentum, volatility, and potential entry/exit points.

COMBINING BOTH ANALYSES

While some traders rely heavily on either fundamental or technical analysis, many successful forex traders use a combination of both. By aligning technical setups with fundamental factors, you can make more informed decisions.

HOW TO BECOME A SUCCESSFUL FOREX TRADER

The following steps are considered crucial and resourceful for becoming successful in forex trading:

CREATING A SOLID TRADING PLAN

A trading plan is a comprehensive strategy that outlines how you will approach the market. A well-defined plan gives you direction and removes emotional decision-making from trading. Here's what your trading plan should include:

Clear Goals: Your plan should begin with clear and measurable goals. Define what you aim to achieve in both the short and long term. Whether you want to achieve a certain return on investment or simply gain experience, having set objectives will keep you focused.

Defined Risk Tolerance: Every trader has a different risk tolerance. Some traders are comfortable with high-risk trades, while others prefer conservative strategies. Knowing how much risk you are willing to take per trade is essential. The general rule is to risk no more than 1-2% of your trading capital on a single trade.

Entry and Exit Criteria: Your plan should clearly define the conditions under which you will enter or exit a trade. This can be based on a combination of technical signals (such as RSI levels or moving average crossovers) or fundamental triggers (such as economic announcements). Sticking to your pre-defined criteria helps remove emotional decisions, which can lead to poor judgment.

Risk-Reward Ratio: Successful traders aim for trades where the potential reward outweighs the risk. A common rule is to maintain a risk-reward ratio of at least 1:2, meaning that for every unit of risk, the potential reward should be twice as large.

EFFECTIVE RISK MANAGEMENT

Risk management is arguably the most critical aspect of becoming a successful forex trader. Without an effective risk management strategy, even the best trading strategies can fail. Here's how to manage your risk effectively:

Use Stop-Loss Orders: A stop-loss order automatically closes a trade when the price reaches a predetermined level. This helps you limit your losses and prevents a single bad trade from wiping out your capital.

Position Sizing: Position sizing refers to determining how much of your capital you will allocate to each trade. As mentioned earlier, successful traders typically risk only a small percentage (1-2%) of their total capital per trade. Position sizing ensures that a losing streak won't have a devastating impact on your account.

Leverage and Margin: Forex trading often involves using leverage, which allows you to control a large position with a small amount of capital. While leverage can magnify profits, it also increases risk. It's crucial to use leverage cautiously and understand its implications fully.

Diversification: Diversification is a risk management technique that involves spreading your investments across different currency pairs. This reduces the impact of a single losing trade or a volatile currency. However, avoid over-diversification, as it can dilute your focus.

EMOTIONAL CONTROL AND DISCIPLINe

Emotions can be a trader's worst enemy. Fear, greed, and impatience can lead to impulsive decisions and significant losses. To be successful in forex trading, you must develop emotional discipline. Here are some disciplinary measures to take:

Avoid Overtrading: Overtrading happens when you execute too many trades within a short period, often due to impatience or the urge to recover losses quickly. Stick to your trading plan and resist the temptation to chase after every potential trade.

Learn to Accept Losses: Losses are inevitable in forex trading, even for the most experienced traders. Accepting losses and learning from them is crucial. Trying to recover losses by making impulsive, high-risk trades usually leads to more significant losses.

Patience is Key: In forex trading, not every day or week will present a perfect trading opportunity. The best traders are those who can wait patiently for the right setups and conditions to enter the market. Discipline and patience go hand in hand.

CONTINUOUS LEARNING AND IMPROVEMENT

The forex market is constantly evolving, influenced by global economic shifts, political events and technological advancements. To stay ahead of the curve, continuous education and self-improvement are essential.

Keep a Trading Journal: A trading journal is a detailed record of every trade you make. It helps you analyze your successes and failures, enabling you to improve your strategies. Over time, patterns will emerge, and you'll gain insights into your trading habits, strengths, and weaknesses.

Stay Updated with Market News: Successful traders stay informed about current events that can impact the forex market. Following financial news, economic reports, and central bank decisions can give you a trading edge.

Engage with the Forex Trading Community: Forex trading communities, whether online forums or social media groups, can provide valuable insights, discussions, and advice. Engaging with experienced traders allows you to learn from their experiences and stay updated with current trends.

To become a successful forex trader is a journey that involves continuous learning, discipline, and strategic thinking. Success in forex is not guaranteed, but with perseverance, a strong work ethic, and the right approach, you can achieve consistent profitability over time. Remember that every great trader started somewhere, and through dedication and discipline, you too can become a successful forex trader.

CHAPTER FIVE

HOW CAN I MANAGE MY FOREX FUNDS EFFECTIVELY?

To manage forex funds effectively is crucial for anyone involved in forex trading. The forex market is known for its high liquidity, accessibility, and potential for substantial profits. However, it is equally known for its volatility and risks, which make fund management essential for long-term success.

Effective fund management involves a combination of risk control, emotional discipline, strategic planning, and sound trading techniques. In this section, we will cover various aspects of how to manage forex funds effectively.

UNDERSTANDING FOREX TRADING AND MARKET DYNAMICS

Before we go into managing forex funds effectively, it's important to understand the basics of the forex market. Forex trading involves the exchange of currencies in pairs, where one currency is bought, and another is sold. The objective is to profit from changes in exchange rates. Forex trading is influenced by numerous factors, including geopolitical events, macroeconomic indicators and market sentiment.

Since forex operates on a global scale, 24 hours a day, it offers opportunities around the clock but also demands careful attention and disciplined fund management. Effective forex fund management hinges on understanding market behavior, tracking trends, and leveraging this knowledge to minimize risk while maximizing profit.

HOW TO MANAGE FOREX FUNDS EFFECTIVELY

The following strategies will help you in managing your forex funds more effectively:

1.   Risk Management

One of the most important aspects of managing forex funds effectively is risk management. The high volatility in the forex market can result in substantial losses, especially for traders who do not employ proper risk management strategies. Risk management involves setting rules and guidelines to limit the amount of money you are willing to loose on any given trade. Some key risk management techniques that every forex trader should adopt include stop-loss orders, position sizing and risk-reward ratio.

2. Diversification

Diversification is a key principle in managing any portfolio, including a forex account. Instead of concentrating all your capital into a single trade or currency pair, diversifying your trades across different currency pairs can reduce the risk of significant losses.

3. Develop a Forex Trading Plan

A trading plan is essential for managing your forex funds effectively. Without a clear plan, traders are more likely to make impulsive decisions driven by emotions, which can result in significant losses. A well-crafted trading plan should include clear trading goals, risk tolerance and capital allocation, entry and exit strategies, time commitment and trading style.

4. Keeping Emotions in Check

One of the biggest challenges in forex trading is managing emotions. Fear and greed can lead to impulsive decisions, such as closing trades too early out of fear of loss or taking excessive risks in the hope of quick profits. Effective forex fund management involves maintaining emotional discipline and sticking to your trading plan, even during periods of market volatility.

5. Using Leverage Responsibly

Leverage is a powerful tool in forex trading, allowing traders to control large positions with a relatively small amount of capital. While leverage can amplify profits, it can also magnify losses, making it essential to use leverage responsibly.

6.   Analyzing Market Trends and Using Technical Analysis

Effective fund management also requires a solid understanding of market analysis. Traders use both technical and fundamental analysis to make informed decisions about when to enter and exit trades. Combining both technical and fundamental analysis can give traders a more comprehensive view of the market and help them make better-informed decisions.

7.   Regularly Reviewing and Adjusting Your Strategy

The forex market is constantly evolving, and what works today may not work tomorrow. As a result, it's essential to regularly review your trading performance and adjust your strategy as needed. This involves analyzing past trades, adapting to market conditions and staying informed

8.   Choosing the Right Forex Broker

Finally, managing your forex funds effectively involves selecting the right forex broker. Your broker is your gateway to the forex market, so it's important to choose one that offers a secure, transparent, and efficient trading environment. When choosing a forex broker, consider the broker's regulation, trading Platform as well as spreads and commissions. In conclusion, managing forex funds effectively is a critical component of long-term success in the forex market.

By implementing the basic principles highlighted in this section, you can protect your capital and increase your chances of profitability.

Effective forex fund management requires discipline, strategy, and continuous improvement. By implementing these techniques and staying informed, traders can optimize returns, minimize losses, and achieve long-term success. Through these combined efforts, you can navigate the complexities of the forex market and manage your funds effectively, paving the way for consistent, sustainable trading success.

CHAPTER SIX

FOREX ACCOUNT MANAGEMENT

It is no news that forex trading in general entails some levels of risks, especially given the technicalities associated with navigating the forex market. The forex market, like some people would describe it can be very brutal, and seemingly harsh to people who lack the needed know-how and level of commitment required to make the most out of situations in the market. Does this mean that people don't succeed in forex? Or to put it in a better way, what options are available to help people succeed in forex trading, while reducing the associated risks to the bearest minimal? Well, that's where forex account management comes to the picture.

This leads to the next question; what is forex account management? What does it entail? How does fund management work? This and lots more is what this section offers. Just stay with me and follow through.

Forex account management refers to the professional service of managing and trading forex accounts on behalf of clients. Let me paint a scenario for better understanding. Imagine an individual who has a case before a court of law. He/she is most likely to employ the service of a lawyer to assist in the case on his/her behalf. The lawyer is well grounded and knowledgeable with regards to matters of litigations or any other issue pertaining to law and the court. The individual may have little to no such knowledge. But by engaging the service of the lawyer in his case, he/she can have some level of confidence knowing that his case would be given professional attention.

Now let's get back to the subject in hand –forex account management. Just like the individual who employed the service of a lawyer who is a professional with regards to legal matters, an individual can equally employ the service of a professional forex trader to help manage and trade his/her forex account in order to better optimize the forex market. In this situation, a professional forex trader manages a client's account by making trades and transactions on behalf of the client for a fee. Forex account management involves forex risks assessments, strategic funds allocation as well as the implementation of forex trading strategies in the client's account in order to achieve goals related to forex trading. So, investors who lack the needed expertise in forex trading but would want to benefit from the windfall in the forex market may consider the option of forex account management.

HOW FUND MANAGEMENT WORKS

As has already been established, forex account management provides an investment opportunity for those who want to leverage the potentials of forex trading by engaging the services of professionals to help manage their accounts. So, how does fund management work? What are the processes involved in forex account management? The process may include, but not limited to the following:

- Setting investment goals
- Risk assessment
- Asset allocation
- Monitoring and adjustment strategies

SETTING CLEAR INVESTMENT GOALS

The first step in funds management would be the establishment or setting of clear investment and trading goals. For this, the forex account manager and client would need to have a clear and mutual understanding so as to establish clear investment objectives which may include income generation, capital growth and even capital preservation among others. In setting clear investment goals, due attention would have to be given to issues relating to profit targets, overall trading strategy, determination of risk tolerance among others. These must be clearly spelt out and agreed upon by both parties involved.

RISK ASSESSMENT

Another key aspect of forex account management revolves around proper assessment as well as management of risks. It is a clearly established fact that the forex market is associated with various risks. It is therefore important for these risks to be properly assessed and efficiently managed. It is on this ground that forex account management becomes a viable option for investors because a professional forex account manager, with his understanding of potential risks, would be better able to navigate through in order to protect the client's capital and also ensure sustainable returns while avoiding losses. With regards to funds management, risk assessment would involve calculating an appropriate position size which is based on the size of the trading account and also the level of risk one is willing to bear on each trade.

ASSET ALLOCATION

Asset allocation in forex account management would entail strategically allocating funds across different currency pairs based on client's preferences and prevalent market conditions. Also, diversification helps with spreading funds across different currency pairs or trading strategies in order to reduce the impact of any single trade on a given account. This further helps to minimize risks and also improve the consistency of trading results.

MONITORING AND ADJUSTMENT STRATEGIES

In order to achieve optimal results with regards to forex account management, it is very crucial to constantly monitor market trends and market performance so as to make very timely decisions and adjustments to trading strategies. This is a continuous process, requiring careful observation and attention of the market environment. Regular review of trading performance helps to assess risk exposures so as to make necessary adjustments so as to adapt to dynamic market conditions.

Other key strategies relating to fund management include stop loss, risk-reward ratio and position sizing

BENEFITS OF FOREX ACCOUNT MANAGEMENT

Beyond reasonable doubts, there are numerous benefits associated with forex account management. Some of these benefits include the following:

i. It offers an opportunity for clients to leverage the expertise and experience of professional forex account managers in efficiently managing their personal accounts.

ii. Forex account management helps clients to save time and efforts by delegating trading responsibilities to professional account managers.

iii. It also helps to reduce the high risks associated with the forex market for clients who employ the service of forex account managers.

CHAPTER SEVEN

HOW TO CHOOSE A GOOD FUND MANAGER

For any investor seeking to optimize their investment portfolio, selecting a good fund manager is a critical decision to make. This decision primarily has the potential of significantly influencing the performance of your investment.

In this section, we will offer an in-depth guide on how to choose a good fund manager for your investment. This will cover essential criteria, methods for evaluation and other tips for making an informed decision.

UNDERSTANDING THE RESPONSIBILITIES OF A GOOD FUND MANAGER

The role of a fund manager revolves around making investment decisions for clients, which may be individuals, an organization or a mutual fund. The main objective is to maximize returns and manage risks based on the investment goals set by the client(s).

A good fund manager will analyze trends in the market, economic indicators and other factors in order to create a diversified portfolio. Let us now consider some of the key factors to look at when choosing a fund manager.

KEY FACTORS TO CONSIDER WHEN CHOOSING A GOOD FUND MANAGER

1. TRACK RECORD AND EXPERIENCE

It is critical to consider these factors when making a choice. The experience of a fund manager is crucial for navigating the complex market. It is important to assess the track record of any manager before investing. A manager with a longer tenure in the market is more likely to make better decisions in the market. As an investor, you should seek reviews and testimonials on a particular manager before committing your investment.

2. QUALIFICATIONS AND CREDENTIALS

You can assess the expertise of a good fund manager by checking his educational background and professional qualifications. Professional certifications such as Chartered Financial Analyst (CFA), Certified Financial Planner (CFP) and Chartered Alternative Investment Analyst (CAIA) are proof of high level professionalism. Also, fund managers who engage in continuous education and training show a commitment to staying updated with market trends and will likely remain relevant.

3. PHILOSOPHY AND INVESTMENT STRATEGY

It is important to understand the investment strategy of a fund manager. This will help to determine if such a strategy is in alignment with your investment goals. You should consider the following:

• **Investment Style:** Different styles adopted by fund managers include growth investing or income focused strategies. Before investing, you should ensure the investment style of the manager aligns with your investment goals.

• **Approach towards Risk Management:** A good fund manager should have a well defined strategy for mitigating losses during volatile periods. You should evaluate the manager's risk management approach within his portfolios.

• **Benchmarking:** You should also check if the manager uses appropriate benchmarks to measure his performance. If he consistently outperforms against relevant benchmarks, that indicates strong skills.

4. FEE STRUCTURE

It is important to understand the fee structure of a particular fund manager you want to invest with. This may have a direct impact on your overall returns. You should consider the following:

• **Total Cost of Investing:** You should consider the total cost of investing with a particular fund manager. This may include administrative fees, trading costs as well as other expenses.

- **Performance Fees:** Some managers usually charge a performance fee based on generated profits. You should understand how such fees are structured and how they may impact your returns.
- **Management Fees**: It is advisable to compare management fees among different fund managers. Those that charge lower fees are usually preferred, however, ensure you don't trade quality for cost.

5. TRANSPARENCY AND COMMUNICATION

Transparency and effective communication are very crucial for fostering a good relationship between a fund manager and his clients. When choosing a fund manager, look out for a manager that provides regular updates on market conditions and overall performance. Also look out for a manager that is transparent. A good manager should be transparent with regards to fees, risks and other operations. It is equally important to evaluate how accessible the fund manager is for consultations and discussions about your investment.

Based on these factors, once you're able to find a good fund manager that meets your consideration, you should conduct the following evaluations.

i. Arrange for an Interview

This will afford you the opportunity to get an insight into the manager's strategies, past performance and overall philosophy. You should prepare questions based on the following key areas:
- The manager's view on risk management and strategies as well.
- How he handles underperforming assets.
- His approach to current market conditions.

You can draw insights from this interview based on the response given. This will enable you to make better informed decisions.

ii. Check for Regulatory Oversight

It is important to ensure the fund manager is duly registered with a relevant regulatory authority. Regulatory compliance by a fund manager gives an added layer of protection. This is to protect you and your investment from potential fraud.

iii. Confirm Performance Reports

Request for detailed performance reports of the manager over different time periods. From the report, you can analyze the manager's returns, comparing it to relevant benchmarks. Also analyze his risk-adjusted performance metrics, as well as consistency in performance across different market cycles.

We cannot overemphasize the importance of choosing a good fund manager. This is paramount for achieving your financial goals. It will be more rewarding when you get a fund manager that understands your investment goals and also meets the requirements with ability to deliver efficiently.

CHAPTER EIGHT

CAN I WITHDRAW MY ACCOUNT FROM MY FUND MANAGER IN FOREX TRADING?

A common question that arises from investors is: "Can I withdraw my account from my fund manager in forex trading?" The answer depends on a range of factors such as the type of agreement between the investor and the fund manager, the terms of the fund, and legal obligations.

The world of forex trading can be incredibly complex, requiring both skill and deep knowledge of global markets. Many investors, rather than managing their forex trades themselves, opt to entrust their funds to professional fund managers. These fund managers, often associated with forex trading firms or hedge funds, make trading decisions on behalf of investors with the aim of generating profits.

This section will comprehensively explore this question, considering different processes involved if you want to withdraw your account from a forex fund manager.

UNDERSTANDING THE ROLE OF A FOREX FUND MANAGER

Before diving into the specifics of fund withdrawals, it is important to understand the role of a forex fund manager. A forex fund manager is a professional or firm that manages investments on behalf of clients. They make trades in the foreign exchange market, aiming to generate returns by speculating on currency pairs and other forex-related financial instruments.

Fund managers use their experience, analytical tools, and market insights to make informed decisions about when to enter or exit trades. They often manage large amounts of capital pooled together from multiple investors, allowing for better diversification and more efficient trading strategies. Some fund managers also employ algorithms or automated trading systems.

CAN I WITHDRAW MY ACCOUNT FROM MY FUND MANAGER?

The short answer is yes, you can typically withdraw your account from your forex fund manager. However, there are numerous factors that determine the process and conditions under which you can do so. Let us now consider these factors that determine if you can withdraw your account from your fund manager. They are as follows:

1. THE NATURE OF YOUR ACCOUNT AGREEMENT

The relationship between you and your forex fund manager is typically governed by a contractual agreement. This agreement outlines the terms and conditions under which the manager will operate, including how much authority they have over your funds, the management fees they charge, and, most importantly, the rules regarding withdrawals. Some of the common types of agreements include:

Managed Accounts: A managed forex account is one in which the investor provides funds for the manager to trade on their behalf, but the investor retains ownership of the account. In this scenario, the investor usually has the right to withdraw funds whenever they choose, subject to specific conditions such as notice periods or withdrawal limits. Managed accounts are often more flexible when it comes to withdrawals.

Pooled Investment Funds: In some cases, your investment may be part of a larger pool of funds managed by the forex manager. In these pooled investment structures (similar to a mutual fund), there may be specific rules governing when and how much of your funds you can withdraw. For example, you may only be able to withdraw during specific redemption periods, which could be quarterly, bi-annually, or annually.

Hedge Funds and Private Investment Vehicles: If your money is managed as part of a hedge fund or private investment vehicle that engages in forex trading, the withdrawal rules are likely to be more restrictive. Many hedge funds enforce lock-up periods, during which investors are not permitted to withdraw their funds. Once the lock-up period expires, there are often specific windows during which you can request withdrawals.

2. NOTICE PERIODS FOR WITHDRAWAL

Many forex fund managers require investors to give advance notice before withdrawing their funds. This is particularly true for pooled investment funds, where the manager may need to liquidate positions or adjust their portfolio to accommodate the withdrawal request.

The notice period can vary depending on the fund or manager. In some cases, it could be as short as 24 to 48 hours, while in other cases, it could be several weeks or even months. The notice period is designed to give the manager enough time to settle trades, prevent undue market disruptions, and avoid negatively affecting other investors in the pool.

3. WITHDRAWAL FEES AND PENALTIES

In addition to notice periods, some fund managers may charge withdrawal fees or penalties for early withdrawals. These fees are often stipulated in the account agreement and may apply under specific circumstances. For example, an early withdrawal during a lock-up period or outside of designated redemption windows could incur a financial penalty. Some of the common withdrawal fees include the following:

Flat Fees: A fixed fee for processing the withdrawal request. This is more common in managed forex accounts, where each withdrawal might be subject to a transaction fee.

Performance Fees: Some fund managers charge performance-based fees, meaning a percentage of the profits generated by the fund is taken as a fee. In cases where investors withdraw funds, they may still be liable for performance fees on profits earned up to the date of withdrawal.

Early Redemption Fees: These fees are particularly common in hedge funds and pooled investment vehicles. If an investor withdraws funds before the agreed-upon redemption period, they might be subject to an early redemption fee. This fee can range from a small percentage to a significant portion of the investment.

4. LIQUIDITY OF INVESTMENTS

The liquidity of the investments made by your forex fund manager also plays a significant role in your ability to withdraw funds. Liquidity refers to how easily assets can be converted into cash. In the forex market, currency pairs are generally highly liquid, meaning that trades can be executed quickly without significantly affecting market prices. However, some forex managers may also invest in less liquid assets or financial instruments such as exotic currency pairs, derivatives, or long-term bonds.

If a significant portion of the fund's capital is tied up in illiquid assets, the manager may impose restrictions on withdrawals to avoid forced liquidations. Forced liquidations can negatively impact the fund's performance and cause losses.

5. PERFORMANCE AND MARKET CONDITIONS

The performance of your fund or managed account can also influence the ease with which you can withdraw your funds. If the fund is performing well and generating profits, the manager is likely to have ample liquidity to accommodate withdrawal requests. However, during periods of poor performance, the fund may experience drawdowns, reducing the available capital for redemptions.

In some extreme cases, fund managers may impose temporary withdrawal restrictions during market downturns or financial crises. This is known as gating, a protective measure that limits withdrawals to avoid a run on the fund. Gating is usually used in hedge funds or pooled investment vehicles and is allowed under the terms of the fund's governing documents.

STEP-BY-STEP PROCESS ON HOW TO WITHDRAW YOUR ACCOUNT FROM YOUR FUND MANAGER

If you've decided to withdraw your funds from your forex fund manager, it's essential to understand the process involved. Here's a general step-by-step guide to withdrawing your account from a forex fund manager:

Step 1: Review the Account Agreement

Before making a withdrawal request, carefully review the terms and conditions outlined in your account agreement or investment prospectus. Pay close attention to any notice periods, fees, and restrictions on withdrawals. This will give you a clear understanding of your rights and the process.

Step 2: Submit a Withdrawal Request

Most fund managers will require you to submit a formal withdrawal request, either through an online platform, email, or a written request. The request should include details such as the amount you wish to withdraw, your account information, and any other necessary documentation.

Step 3: Wait for the Notice Period (If Applicable)

If your fund agreement requires a notice period, you will need to wait for the specified time before your withdrawal can be processed. During this period, the manager may adjust the portfolio or settle trades to free up the necessary liquidity.

Step 4: Withdrawal Fees or Penalties (If Applicable)

Depending on the terms of your agreement, the manager may deduct any applicable fees or penalties before transferring the remaining funds to your account. Be sure to clarify what fees might be applied and how they are calculated.

Step 5: Receive Your Funds

Once the withdrawal request has been processed and any notice period has passed, the funds will be transferred to your designated bank account or payment method. The time it takes for the funds to appear in your account will vary based on the manager's procedures and your bank's processing times.

CHAPTER NINE

HOW PROFITABLE IS FOREX COPY TRADING INVESTMENT

Forex copy trading investment has become popular, especially for those who want to venture into trading without the need for extensive market knowledge or experience. In recent years, it has afforded traders the ability of earning passive income in the financial market.

This investment strategy is also referred to as social trading or mirror trading. It basically makes forex trading accessible to a wider audience and reduces the need for extensive market analysis and technical knowledge. In this section, we will explore this investment strategy, particularly highlighting some of the factors that determine its profitability. However, before we proceed, let us quickly have an overview of this trading strategy.

OVERVIEW OF FOREX COPY TRADING INVESTMENT

Forex copy trading is a trading investment/trading strategy that allows traders to copy and replicate the trades of more experienced traders. The concept is quite easy. An experienced trader with a proven track record is selected, and his trades are automatically mirrored in the account of the copy trader. In some cases, multiple copy traders can equally copy the trades of a master trader simultaneously.

Basically, this approach leverages the skills of seasoned traders to create opportunities for less experienced investors. It is a passive way of engaging the forex market, yet making gains at the same time from the market. Given its potential for profit without requiring deep financial expertise, forex copy trading investment appeals to the interest of many traders. This appeal lies in the fact that anyone can participate in Forex markets without needing to analyze charts, economic indicators, or market sentiment.

HOW DOES COPY TRADING WORKS

Here's a quick rundown of how copy trading works:

- The trader who wishes to copy a signal provider is expected to first select a trading platform or broker that offers copy trading services to open an account with. Note that copy trading requires a powerful trading platform.
- Once a platform or broker has been selected and account opened, the copy trader needs to register, verify and fund the account.
- Next to the account set up would be finding successful traders (signal provider) to follow and copy their trades. This is an important step because the level of profit a copy trader would reach to a large extent would depend on the signal provider being followed. Therefore it is important that the copy trader follows and copies top rated traders so as to ensure some level of safety.
- Once a signal provider has been selected and followed, the copy trader can allocate a portion of his capital and start copying the signal provider. He can also start monitoring his trade performance and all.

FEATURES OF FOREX COPY TRADING INVESTMENT

This investment strategy has several unique features that enhance the user experience and facilitate effective trading. Its features include the following:

i. Automated Trading

Automation is one of the most attractive features of the forex copy trading investment. Once you select a trader to copy, the system handles all the execution of trades, allowing for a hands-off approach.

ii. Diversification

This strategy allows investors to copy multiple traders at once, thereby spreading their capital across different strategies and currency pairs. This diversification can reduce risk and enhance potential returns.

iii. Performance Tracking

Most platforms provide detailed statistics on traders' performance, including historical returns, risk levels, and win rates. This data helps investors make informed decisions about whom to follow.

iv. Flexibility

Investors can adjust their investments based on changing market conditions or the performance of the traders they are copying. They can stop copying a trader at any time or switch to another one if desired.

v. Community Engagement

Many platforms foster a community where traders share insights, strategies, and updates. This collaborative environment can be beneficial for learning and networking.

At this point, we can now consider the factors that determine the profitability of this investment strategy.

FACTORS THAT DETERMINE THE PROFITABILITY OF FOREX COPY TRADING INVESTMENT

i. Selection of Trader to Copy

Selecting a successful trader to copy is perhaps the most crucial that influences the success of copy trading. Investors need to analyze past performance, risk levels, and trading styles. Look for traders with a consistent track record, low drawdown periods, and a clear risk management strategy. A trader with a consistent track record may yield better results, and is more reliable compared to one with sporadic successes.

ii. Market Conditions

The profitability of forex copy trading investment can be significantly influenced by market conditions. This is because the overall market environment plays a vital role in overall profitability. Therefore, factors such as Economic events, market sentiment and geopolitical factors can easily influence currency movements and therefore, profitability. However, Traders having the ability to adapt to changing conditions are more likely to remain profitable. This again further buttresses the need to make the right selection of a trader to copy.

iii. Capital Allocation

The amount of capital an investor allocates to forex copy trading investment can significantly influence the overall profitability. Some traders may make the mistake of either allocating too little, or too allocating too much to a single trader. Allocating too little may lead to minimal returns, while allocating too much to a single trader can increase risk. You need to find a middle position between these two extremes in order to profit significantly from investing in forex copy trading.

iv. Risk Management

Effective risk management is essential for maximizing profits, or at least, minimizing losses, because even the best traders experience losses. It's essential that traders understand the risks associated with copy trading and implement appropriate risk management techniques, such as setting stop-loss orders and portfolio diversification. Investors should also consider their own risk tolerance when choosing traders to copy.

v. Trading Platform

The quality of the Forex copy trading platform is another important factor that can enhance overall profitability. Some of the features a good platform should have include reliability, ease of use, and a good number of traders available for copying. On this note, it's important to point out that copy trading platforms charge various fees. All of which may have certain impacts on overall profitability.

DIFFERENCES BETWEEN COPY TRADING AND THE TRADITIONAL TRADING

Below are some of the areas where the copy trading strategy differs from the traditional trading:

i. Whereas the traditional trading involves making buys and sells in the market based on individual market analysis and research, copy trading involves automatically replicating the trades of other experienced traders.

ii. A high level of understanding of the market is required for traditional trading, whereas copy trading can be suitable for individuals who may not have extensive trading experience.

iii. Traditional trading requires that individual traders make their own decisions with regards to what, when and how to trade. For copy trading on the other hand, such decisions are handed over to the signal provider.

iv. Traditional trading requires more involvement and personal management of the individual, whereas copy trading requires less daily management once a signal provider has been chosen and copied.

v. Traditional traders need to personally develop strategies for spreading risks and managing portfolios, but copy traders may diversify by copying different traders so as to spread risks across different strategies.

CHAPTER TEN

PROS AND CONS OF FOREX COPY TRADING

Forex copy trading has become a very popular trading strategy among traders. This is as a result of various reasons, which include its potential for high liquidity, accessibility and potential for substantial profit.

It is a known fact that forex trading in general can be daunting for beginners as it requires extensive knowledge, accurate market analysis and emotional resilience. It is for this cause that forex copy trading has emerged to bridge this gap and make trading the forex market more accessible to beginners and experienced traders alike.

Like with any other human endeavor, forex copy trading has its pros and cons. The major focus of this section is to shed light on the pros and cons of forex copy trading, providing enlightenment on the subject matter, and helping readers to make better informed decisions.

PROS OF FOREX COPY TRADING

Highlighted below are some of the pros of forex copy trading:

i. Accessibility, especially for beginners

This is one of the major benefits of forex copy trading, especially to those that are new to the forex environment. Given that learning and understanding the rudiments of forex for starters can be a really daunting and challenging task. It can take a really long time for beginners to learn the basics of trading and understand movements in the market. But forex copy trading comes to the rescue, granting beginners access to the forex market by leveraging the knowledge and expertise of other experienced traders. So, instead of trying and failing, a beginner can easily copy the trades and strategies of others. This way, he stands a chance of making profits, and also learning on the go.

ii. Saves Time

The traditional forex trading strategy usually demands long hours of making research, analyses, studying charts and keeping up with market trends. Forex copy trading saves traders the time that would have been otherwise spent on the above listed demands. This is even more beneficial to traders who have a full time job or some other engagements. This way, such individuals can have the time to attend to those engagements and still benefit from trading forex.

iii. Potential for Higher Returns

Forex copy trading affords traders very high chances of getting higher returns and profits. This is very simple because you get to select traders you wish to copy. If the traders you copy are successful in their trades, chances are you also make the same success from your own end. The more successful traders you copy, the more your chances of having successful trades, thereby yielding you higher returns.

iv. Diversification

Given that forex copy trading allows for a trader to copy multiple traders, it can help the trader in portfolio diversification. Very often, most of the different traders that are being copied have their different strategies and approach to the market. By incorporating these different strategies, traders can create a diversified portfolio without having to manually search for trades themselves.

v. Learning Opportunities

Another benefit of forex copy trading is that it offers traders the opportunity to learn on the go. In the course of following and copying successful traders, one can learn from their strategies and build experience. So as a forex copy trader, you get to learn while you earn.

CONS OF FOREX COPY TRADING

Below are some of the cons of forex copy trading:

i. Fees and Extra Charges

Some of the fees charged by some copy trading platforms can actually eat into your profits overtime. Some platforms even charge a fixed commission on profits and per trade that is copied. These charges may come in different forms and can add up overtime to become enormous.

ii. Increased Dependency

Despite the convenience associated with this trading strategy, one of its major bad sides is that it creates a level of dependency on others. It places you at the mercy of the traders you copy, making you lose your own unique touch and input in trades.

iii. Limited Control

This is closely related to the previous point. Engaging in copy trades makes you relinquish a significant amount of control over your trades. The traders you copy exercise a greater level of control than you do. Consequently, your profits or losses are significantly dependent on the decisions they make.

iv. Exposure to Risks

Copy traders are not immune to risks. As a matter of fact, depending on the traders they copy, they may even be more exposed to risks. For example, if the trader being copied experiences losses in a given trade, the losses can equally be experienced by those copying his trades.

CHAPTER ELEVEN

CAN I ADJUST LEVERAGE WHEN COPY TRADING?

One of the key questions that is popular among traders is "can I adjust leverage when copy trading?" Copy trading provides the ability to participate in markets without needing in-depth knowledge of trading strategies. Leverage is an essential concept in trading, allowing traders to control a large position with a relatively small amount of capital.

This section explores the role of leverage in copy trading, the flexibility (or limitations) in adjusting leverage when copy trading, and the implications it has for your trading experience.

WHAT IS LEVERAGE IN TRADING?

Leverage is a mechanism that allows traders to borrow funds from the broker to increase their exposure in the market. Essentially, it amplifies your trading position relative to your actual capital. For example, if a trader has $1,000 and uses a leverage of 1:100, they can control a position of $100,000.

While leverage can magnify profits, it also increases the potential for losses. This is why understanding leverage is crucial, especially in the context of copy trading where your account is following another trader's moves.

HOW DOES LEVERAGE WORK IN COPY TRADING?

Leverage remains important when engaging in copy trading because:

• Expert traders or signal providers often use leverage to enhance their potential returns.

• As a copy trader, your account replicates the exact trades of the expert trader, including the leverage applied.

For example, if the expert trader enters a position with 1:30 leverage, your account will generally mirror that leverage, unless the platform you are using allows for customization.

However, the extent to which you can adjust leverage in copy trading depends largely on the platform and broker policies. Some platforms allow you to tweak certain parameters, including leverage, while others maintain a direct, unalterable copy of the expert trader's settings.

CAN YOU ADJUST LEVERAGE WHEN COPY TRADING?

The ability to adjust leverage when copy trading is not universally available. Different copy trading platforms have varying levels of control, and understanding these nuances is key. Here are some of the popular copy trading platforms and their policies relating to this:

1. eToro: This is one of the most well-known copy trading platforms, and it provides some level of customization. However, when you copy a trader, the leverage they use is generally applied to your trades as well. You cannot individually adjust the leverage on a trade-by-trade basis when copy trading on eToro. The leverage is dictated by the trader you are copying.

2. ZuluTrade: This offers more flexibility when it comes to managing risk. While you copy a trader's strategy, you can adjust the size of the copied trade relative to your own capital. This indirectly affects leverage, but there is no specific option to manually adjust the leverage for each individual trade.

3. MetaTrader 4/5 Copy Trading: On MetaTrader platforms, when using the copy trading feature, the settings of the signal provider are mirrored, including leverage. However, you can adjust the percentage of your equity that you want to allocate to copying a trader. In terms of leverage adjustment, this is typically managed at the account level with your broker rather than within individual trades.

4. cTrader: cTrader's copy trading function provides a more flexible structure where you can adjust the "copy ratio" in relation to the provider's trades. The leverage, however, is still generally tied to the original trader's settings unless you have predefined risk management measures in place.

FACTORS AFFECTING LEVERAGE ADJUSTMENT

Several factors can influence whether or not you can adjust leverage when copy trading. This includes the following:

1. Regulatory Restrictions: Some regions, such as the European Union under ESMA regulations, limit the amount of leverage retail traders can use. This may affect your ability to increase leverage when copying trades.

2. Broker Policies: Brokers may impose their own restrictions on leverage depending on the account type and asset class. For instance, leverage on forex may be higher compared to leverage on indices or stocks.

3. Signal Provider's Settings: In most cases, the signal provider or expert trader's use of leverage is mirrored in your account. This means that if the trader uses high leverage, your account will follow suit, unless you employ specific risk management tools.

BENEFITS OF ADJUSTING LEVERAGE WHILE COPY TRADING

1. Control over Risk: Being able to adjust leverage gives you greater control over the amount of risk you're taking on each trade. Lower leverage means less exposure, reducing the potential for significant losses.

2. Customizable Trading Experience: Some traders prefer higher leverage to amplify profits, while others may want to keep risk low. Having the flexibility to adjust leverage allows traders to customize their copy trading experience according to their risk tolerance.

3. Enhanced Returns: Traders who are more confident in their signal provider's performance may want to increase leverage to maximize potential returns.

HOW TO MANAGE RISK WHILE COPY TRADING

Even if you cannot adjust leverage directly, there are several ways to manage risk while copy trading. These are as follows:

• **Allocate a Smaller Percentage of Your Capital:** Rather than using all your available funds, allocate only a portion of your capital to copy trading. This limits your exposure and helps manage overall risk.

• **Set Stop-Loss Limits:** Many copy trading platforms allow you to set a stop-loss limit on your account. If the total drawdown reaches a predefined level, the system will stop copying trades, helping to protect your capital.

• **Diversify Your Copy Portfolio:** Copying multiple traders with different strategies can help you diversify your risk. Some traders may use high leverage, while others may take a more conservative approach. Diversification can help balance your risk exposure.

• **Monitor the Performance of Signal Providers:** Keep a close eye on the performance of the traders you are copying. If their strategy changes or they start taking excessive risks, you can stop copying them or adjust your portfolio.

The question of whether you can adjust leverage when copy trading depends heavily on the platform you are using. Some platforms offer more flexibility, allowing you to indirectly control leverage through tools like copy ratios and equity allocation, while others strictly mirror the leverage used by the signal provider.

It's important to remember that while leverage can amplify profits, it also increases potential losses. Before attempting to adjust leverage in copy trading, ensure you understand the risks and the strategies of the traders you are copying. Additionally, using risk management tools, such as stop-loss settings and diversification, can help mitigate the risks associated with leverage.

CHAPTER TWELVE

METATRADER COPIER: HOW MT4 & MT5 COPY TRADING WORK

The Meta Trader copier is a powerful tool which is very essential in the world of forex trading. Understanding how MT4 and MT5 copy trading works is of absolute necessity to those who intend to engage in copy trading. Before we fully launch into the focus of this section, let's understand what the Meta Trader actually is. We will also look into MT4 and MT5, and of course, how copy trading works on these platforms.

EXPLANATION OF THE META TRADER

Forex trading entails quite a lot of things that facilitates its effectiveness. One of such things is a trading platform. There are different trading platforms on which forex trading is executed by a vast number of traders and brokers. One such trading platform is the Meta Trader. This is a very popular trading platform that offers both investors and retail traders access to derivatives, commodities and stocks in major markets, which include forex trading, cryptocurrencies and CFDs. The Meta Trader is developed by MetaQuotes Software Corporation and provides a sophisticated technological infrastructure for brokers and traders who can take advantage of its incredible features which include market analysis algorithms, advanced charting packages, multiple indicator systems, among others. The Meta Trader has afforded brokers, and indeed the financial service industry at large convenience and almost everything that is required to efficiently carry out their operations in the global financial market.

The Meta Trader copier makes it possible for investors to replicate successful trading strategies across different trading accounts, given its flexibility, control and ability to streamline trade replication to meet the specific needs of different traders. The Meta Trader essentially allows traders in the forex trading environment to copy and replicate trading strategies from one Meta Trader account (usually referred to as the signal provider or expert trader) to another Meta Trader account (usually referred to as the copier).

MT4 AND MT5

The MT4 (Meta Trader 4) and MT5 (Meta Trader 5) are both official versions of the Meta Trader platform created and distributed by the MetaQuotes Software Corporation. They both have certain similarities and differences which are highlighted below:

SIMILARITIES BETWEEN MT4 AND MT5

Some of the major similarities between MT4 and MT5 include the following:

1. Both the MT4 and MT5 platforms use a similar user interface having similar toolbars, customizable charts and windows. They both facilitate automated trading, technical analysis, and provide access to trading services.

2. They both have market watch windows that allow traders to track live price quotes of different financial instruments.

3. Both the MT4 and MT5 platforms allow multiple order types including pending orders, market orders, take-profit and stop-loss orders.

4. The MT4 and MT5 are both available both as mobile apps for Android and IOS and as web based versions.

DIFFERENCES BETWEEN MT4 AND MT5

Below are some of the observable differences between the MT4 and MT5

1. While MT4 is basically designed for forex trading, with a strong focus on currency pairs (although it supports trading in a limited number of other financial instruments), MT5 has a wider coverage, support trading in forex commodities as well as other financial instruments.

2. MT4 uses the MQL4 programming language which is suitable for simpler trading algorithms, whereas MT5 uses the MQL5 programming language which is suitable for more complex trading algorithms and advanced backtesting.

3. Another difference between both platforms is that the MT4 platform supports 4 types of pending orders. These buy limit, sell limit, buy stop and sell stop. On the other hand, the MT5 platform supports 2 extra types of pending orders in addition to the ones supported by MT4. These are buy stop limit and sell stop limit.

4. Whereas the MT4 platform offers 9 timeframes which ranges from one minute to one month, the MT5 platform offers 12 additional timeframes to the ones offered by MT4, making it a total of 21 timeframes offered by MT5.

HOW MT4 & MT5 COPY TRADING WORK

We can now give a detailed rundown of how copy trading works on both the MT4 and MT5 trading platforms. This has been itemized in a few steps given below:

Step1. Select a Signal Provider

Signal providers refer to the expert traders who offer their trading strategies and activities for others to copy and replicate. On both platforms, signal providers are usually rated based on certain metrics including their trading performance, number of subscribers and risk levels.

Step2. Subscription

Haven selected a signal provider, the next step is to subscribe to their signals. This can be accessed through the 'signal tab' in both the MT4 and MT5 platforms. This may involve paying a subscription fee and agreeing to the terms of the signal provider.

Step3. Parameters set-up

Things to consider under this step include adjustment of trade size, risk management and synchronization. The trade size of the copied trade can be adjusted to suit an individual's risk tolerance. This is usually set as a fraction of the signal provider's trade size. Options for risk management on MT4 and MT5 copy trading include maximum drawdown, stop-loss levels and limits on the number of trades to copy. Next, is account synchronization that allows a trader's account to be synchronized with the account of the signal provider such that the trading activities of the signal provider can be opened in the account of the copier.

Step4. Execute and Monitor

Once the set up has been properly done, automatically the trades of the signal provider gets replicated and executed on the copier's account, including necessary adjustments. The MT4 and MT5 platforms allow copiers to monitor the performance of copy trades with provision to make certain adjustments in real time.

Step5. Ending a Subscription

One can equally decide to stop copying and subscribing to a signal provider and can choose to either retain or close existing positions. After ending a subscription the trader can exercise full control of the trades that are remaining.

Summarily, both the MT4 and MT5 copy traders are powerful platforms that facilitate copy trading experience for both beginners and expert traders. The MT5 platform however possesses more advanced features which gives it an edge over the MT4 platform.

CHAPTER THIRTEEN

HOW PROFITABLE IS FOREX PAMM INVESTMENT

Forex is one of the most dynamic financial markets and forex PAMM investment has become really popular among traders and investors in the forex market. This investment strategy involves entrusting your funds to experienced forex traders who manage a pooled account, allocating trades based on predetermined percentages.

Forex PAMM investment offers a wealth of opportunities for profit to traders. This is because it gives an opportunity to gain massively from the market without the need for extensive technical knowledge or time commitment.

This section seeks to fully explore the profitability of the forex PAMM investment. It shall however highlight some other important features to provide a better understanding of the subject in hand.

UNDERSTANDING FOREX PAMM INVESTMENT

This stands for Percentage Allocation Management Module. It allows investors the ability to allocate their funds to a professional trader (fund manager). The manager then uses the collective pool of funds to trade in the Forex market. Profits or losses are distributed in proportion to the amount of capital each investor has contributed to the account.

Investors can easily track the performance of their selected PAMM managers and withdraw their funds when they choose. This is usually based on the terms of a specific investment period.

One good thing about this method is that investors do not need a full understanding of the intricacies of Forex trading. They rather rely on the expertise of professional traders.

HOW PAMM ACCOUNTS WORK

Before we dive fully into the main focus of this section, which is the profitability of forex PAMM investment, let us quickly explain how this system works. Here is a quick rundown of how this strategy works:

i. Selection of PAMM Manager

It begins with selecting a manager or different managers. Different PAMM managers have their different performance history, trading strategy and profit-sharing model. Also, most brokers that offer PAMM services usually rank managers based on past performance, risk profile, and other criteria. This way, investors can easily browse through to make a selection of a manager based on their preferences.

ii. Capital Pooling

Different investors usually combine their funds with the trader's own capital, which the trader uses to run trades. The share of profits or losses allocated to each investor is usually determined by the size of each investor's contribution.

iii. Profit Allocation

Using the pooled capital from the investors, the trader takes forex trades. As expected, the profits or losses from the trades are distributed among the investors based on their contribution percentage.

iv. Performance Fee

PAMM managers usually charge a performance fee, which is a percentage of the profit generated. This could serve as incentives to the traders to perform well, as they only earn if they deliver profits for their investors.

FACTORS AFFECTING THE PROFITABILITY OF FOREX PAMM INVESTMENT

The following are some of the major factors that determine how profitable the forex PAMM investment is.

1. Trading Skill of the Manager

The profitability of forex PAMM investment is largely determined by the expertise of the trader managing the funds. This is like the most crucial factor for profit. The more experienced and skilled a PAMM manager is, the higher his potential to generate consistent returns, even in volatile market conditions. Successful traders use strategies that combine technical analysis, risk management, and fundamental insights to capitalize on market movements. Poorly managed PAMM accounts may result in losses, underscoring the importance of choosing the right manager.

2. Market Conditions

The Forex market is highly volatile, and market conditions can significantly impact the profitability of PAMM investments. Low volatility in the market may result in smaller profit margins, as it gives traders less opportunities to capitalize on price swings. On the other hand, high volatility can offer more opportunities, but however bear higher risks.

A skilled PAMM manager can adapt very well to market conditions and adjust their strategy accordingly. For instance, during high volatility, some managers may employ aggressive strategies. Others may adopt more conservative approaches during uncertain market conditions.

3. Risk Management

Another major factor that influences profitability is the risk management techniques employed by the PAMM manager. Effective risk management practices are essential for protecting investors' capital and for mitigating losses. While some riskier managers may yield higher returns, their potential for losses might be even greater. The account manager's ability to manage risk through techniques like stop-loss orders and position sizing can significantly influence profitability.

4. Investment Strategy

The investment strategy adopted by the account manager is also crucial in determining the profitability of the investment. A well-defined strategy that aligns with the investor's risk tolerance and investment goals can enhance profitability.

Haven explored the major factors that determine the profitability of the forex PAMM investment, let's see some of its advantages.

ADVANTAGES OF FOREX PAMM INVESTMENT

i. Hands-Free Investment

This unique trading strategy offers investors a hands-free investment. You don't need to actively engage in day-to-day trading decisions. Everything is done by the PAMM manager, from market analysis to trade execution. This makes it an ideal option for those who want exposure to Forex markets without the stress of trading.

ii. Diversification

Many PAMM accounts are usually diversified across various currencies and trading strategies. This further reduces the impact of a single bad trade or strategy, and also increases the overall stability and potential profitability of the investment.

iii. Risk Management

The account manager is incentivized to employ prudent risk management strategies. This is because his own capital is also invested alongside the capitals of the investors. This alignment of interests helps ensure that the manager takes calculated risks rather than speculative bets.

CHAPTER FOURTEEN

WHAT TO CONSIDER WHEN CHOOSING A PAMM MANAGER

For various reasons, choosing a PAMM manager can be quite a daunting task. It can even get worse when you don't know what to look out for in making your selection. In the dynamic world of forex trading, as in any other endeavor, finding the right tools and strategies is crucial for ensuring success. One of the most effective strategies investors with limited time or experience are utilizing for succeeding in forex is choosing a PAMM manager.

This section seeks to guide you through the key factors to consider when choosing a PAMM manager. Here, we'll break down the factors and important features to look out for before making your investment.
Before we proceed however, we will have a quick rundown of who a PAMM manager is.

WHO IS A PAMM MANAGER?

Firstly, PAMM here is an acronym for Percentage Allocation Management Module. It is an account that allows investors to allocate their capital to a professional trader, who manages and trades the funds on their behalf, distributing profits (and losses) proportionally. Given this explanation, A PAMM manager is a professional trader who manages a pool of funds for investors.

If you're considering investing in a PAMM account, it's crucial to choose a manager who aligns with your investment goals and risk tolerance. It's important to note that making the wrong choice could lead to significant losses, while a well-chosen manager can maximize your returns.
Let us now highlight some of the main factors you should consider when choosing a PAMM manager.

FACTORS TO CONSIDER WHEN CHOOSING A PAMM MANAGER
These include the following:

- Track record and experience
- Regulatory compliance
- Risk management strategy
- Fees and cost
- Reputation and reviews
- Withdrawal policy

i. Track Record and Experience

Experience is one of the most critical factors to consider when choosing a PAMM manager. This is because an experienced PAMM manager will have a history of navigating different market conditions and consistently delivering profitable returns. Beyond the returns however, the consistency of the manager is another key consideration. It is therefore important to assess the track record to ensure the manager has been consistent for a substantial period. A manager's past performance is a strong indicator of their future potential. The ability of a manager to deliver stable returns in both volatile and stable markets is a proof of efficiency and reliability, especially when compared to those who show sporadic large profits punctuated by substantial losses. Summarily, when looking at a manager's experience and track record, your checks should be channeled towards ability to adapt to varying market conditions, length of time trading under PAMM, historical performance over time, including both profits and losses, among other considerations.

ii. Regulatory compliance

This is another important factor to check. Be sure that the manager is subject to regulatory oversight by a reputable authority. This is in order to protect your investments. In this regard, you should verify that the manager holds the necessary licenses and permits to operate in your region. Verify to be sure that the manager complies with relevant laws and regulations, including anti-money laundering and know-your-customer (KYC) requirements. Also, be sure to understand how the manager manages risks, such as market volatility, liquidity, and credit risk.

iii. Risk management strategy

Although a PAMM manager may boast impressive returns, if they are achieved through reckless risk-taking, this may imply danger for your investments. Understanding how a PAMM manager handles risk is very important. This is because risk management is a crucial aspect of successful trading. It is therefore advisable to look for a manager who strictly adheres to risk control measures. These measures may include limiting leverage, using stop-loss orders, and diversification across different assets. Also consider the manager's drawdown. A manager having a low maximum drawdown is generally safer because he can maintain risk within acceptable limits. High drawdowns on the other hand suggest that the manager is employing high-risk strategies. This has the potential of wiping out significant portions of your investment during market downturns.

iv. Fees and cost

When choosing a PAMM manager, understanding the fee structure is very critical to your bottom line. PAMM managers usually charge a performance fee based on profits generated. This fee is a percentage of the profits, which can range from 10% to 50% or more, depending on the manager's reputation and track record. Some managers however also charge management fees regardless of the performance. This could erode investor's profits if the manager does not perform well. It is therfore important to ensure that the fee structure aligns with your   expectations. Generally, a performance based fee is more favorable, as it ties the manager's success to your returns. It is good practice that a PAMM manager be incentivized to protect your investment and make consistent profits, not merely collect fees.

v. Reputation and reviews

You can get an additional insight into the effectiveness and trustworthiness of a manager based on his reputation. You should look for reviews and feedback from other investors who have used the PAMM manager's services. You can also gather information about a manager's history with clients via online forums, review sites, and social media.

Although reviews may be subjective, consistent feedback from multiple sources (either positive or negative) is worth noting. Be cautious of fake reviews; always verify that the reviews and feedback are authentic.

vi. Withdrawal policy

It is also important to consider the withdrawal policy associated with your PAMM account when choosing a PAMM manager. While some managers may offer flexible terms, allowing you to withdraw at any time without fees, others may have lock-in periods. During such periods, you cannot withdraw your funds, or they may impose penalties for early withdrawals. So, understanding how accessible your funds are is very vital when choosing a PAMM manager.

CHAPTER FIFTEEN

HOW TO BECOME A FOREX PAMM MANAGER

Many people are increasingly indicating interest in becoming a forex PAMM manager. This can be attributed to the fact that forex PAMM account management is gradually gaining massive attention in the forex space. While this can be promising and has potentials of yielding good returns, it is important to get the processes right.

Any individuals who wish to become a forex PAMM manager should be able to ask the right questions, get the right answers. In essence, get the right information. This is more like the first step in the right direction.

"How can I become a forex PAMM manager?" If this question reflects what you have in your mind, then this is right for you. This section is all about sharing valuable insights that will help provide the right answers to the above questions. It will also serve as a guide, offering step by step direction on the processes involved in becoming a profitable forex PAMM manager.

WHAT DOES A FOREX PAMM MANAGER DO?

To effectively function in a given role or position, it is imperative to fully understand the demands of the role. You stand a chance to be a better forex PAMM manager when you have a better understanding of what they do.

A forex PAMM manager can also be referred to as a forex account manager or account controller. Basically, the job here revolves around the management of forex trading accounts of investors. In most cases, the manager receives pooled funds from different investors, and uses the funds to execute trades on behalf of the investors.

STEPS IN BECOMING A FOREX PAMM MANAGER

Let's look at a step by step overview of how to become a forex PAMM manager.

Step One: Gather Knowledge and Build Experience in Forex Trading

To become a profitable forex account manager, you have to know your onions well with regards to forex trading. Have a profound understanding of forex trading, market analysis and risk management strategies in the forex market. Become proficient in trading forex. When this is achieved, your results will speak on your behalf. Investors will feel confident in your performance, and can even recommend you to other investors.

Step Two: Establish a Proven Track Record in Trading

This is a quick follow up on the first step. Haven gotten enough understanding of forex trading, the next is to establish yourself as a profitable trader. How do you go about this? You have to build a reputable track record that will make potential investors trust you enough to commit their funds for you to manage. Build and show a consistent trading history and performance with time. Consistency is key. For investors to be attracted to your PAMM account, they need to be convinced that you can deliver on the job. They need to see proof that you can effectively manage risks, and most importantly, generate good returns on their investments.

Step Three: Get Required Licensing

To successfully operate a PAMM service, you may be required to get certain licenses and approval by some regulatory authorities. This may differ based on location, but is however important. This further validates your service and gives potential investors a certain level of trust in your service.

Step Four: Get a Forex Broker

When making a selection for a forex broker there are certain factors you should consider. You definitely want to get a broker that offers a platform for PAMM account services. He should have a good reputation, as well as a reliable platform. Understand his fee structures and charges, spreads offered and level of regulatory compliance among other factors. These checks will help you have a better experience in managing your PAMM account.

Step Five: Open a PAMM Account

Haven gotten a reputable broker, open a PAMM account and proceed with the required verification and other processes. Set up the PAMM account so you can begin to manage funds from investors. You may also set up other structures like performance fee, investment amount and even profit-loss sharing ratio.

Step Six: Create a Trading Strategy

Clearly define your trading strategy and follow through with it consistently. Remember that your strategy should be profitable and well proven by your own performance. You can equally include your risk management rules, trading frequency and assets you trade on.

Step Seven: Market Your Service

The goal is to attract enough investors to invest in your PAMM account. You can do this by effectively promoting your PAMM management offering. You can use your broker's platform and other forums to achieve this. You can equally create a professional website and even utilize social media platforms.

Step Eight: Have an Effective Risk Management Strategy

Implement effective risk management practices. You may want to include strategies such as diversification, stop-loss orders, position sizing, etc. These strategies should help minimize losses and protect investors' funds. It is also important to always maintain clear communication with investors.

Step Nine: Stay Updated

Ensure to stay updated and follow up with trends in the forex markets. The forex market is very dynamic and is subject to various fluctuations.

In order to make the most of market situations, you need to frequently monitor the market, redefine your strategies at some point, and make other adjustments when necessary. To be a successful forex PAMM manager, you have to maintain top performance level and remain competitive.

The process of becoming a successful forex PAMM manager may not be very smooth and easy. However, following the guides offered in this article, you are sure to be on your way to actualizing this goal.

CHAPTER SIXTEEN

HOW TO ATTRACT INVESTORS FOR MY PAMM ACCOUNTS AS A TRADER

Obviously, how to attract investors for my PAMM account would be my major goal as a trader offering the services of a PAMM account manager. The very essence of running a PAMM account is not just for me. It is not just for the fun of doing it. It is rather for the value I intend to offer through it. And the primary recipients of the value are investors.

Based on this premise, attracting investors for my PAMM account becomes a major objective. I am therefore expected to consciously put in efforts, and strategically devise means to attract as many investors as possible.

The aim of this section is to offer insights and valuable information that will assist traders acquire the relevant skills for attracting investors for their PAMM accounts. This may not be a very easy venture. But getting the right information will always be an advantage. Information they say is power. That is exactly what this section seeks to equip you with -power to successfully attract investors to your PAMM account.

STEPS TO ATTRACT INVESTORS FOR YOUR PAMM ACCOUNT

At this point, we can now walk through the steps and processes involved in attracting investors for your PAMM account. Here is a detailed step-by-step guide, highlighting the processes for achieving this objective:

Step One: Develop an Impressive Trading Track Record

There's always something about having an impressive track record in what you do. It has a way of shutting certain oppositions and repelling doubts. This is also applicable in forex trading, especially, when it comes to trying to attract investors for your PAMM account. You should develop a verifiable history with impressive trading performance over time. Investors are interested in traders who can yield steady and profitable returns. And if you can convince them of your ability to perform, then you are right on your way to attract as many investors.

Step Two: Provide Detailed Reports on your Trading Performance

People are more convinced by what they see relative to what they hear. This is in support of the popular axiom -seen is believing. You can easily talk about your excellent performances in forex trading and all. But 'telling' won't do as much as 'showing' would. That is why it is important to provide very detailed reports on your trading performance. Ensure to publish your trading reports regularly. Your report should include risk management practices, trading statistics as well as returns and profits made. Providing this report proves to potential investors that you are profitable and their investment can be safe with you.

Step Three: Establish a Professional Presence Online

In order to attract investors for your PAMM account, you need to establish a strong and professional online presence. People need to know you and what you offer. They need to see the value you provide. You can't attract investors enough if you are hidden. To achieve online visibility, you can create a professional website to showcase your PAMM account offerings, performance and testimonials. You can also leverage social media platforms to actively engage potential investors. In growing your online presence, you should seek endorsement and testimonials from other existing investors. Recommendations from other investors can also play a vital role in pushing your online presence.

Step Four: Engage in Active Networking and Marketing

It is important to network with other members of the forex trading community. Engage with forex trading forums, participate in online activities and events. Build valuable relationships that will grant you some level of exposure. This can go a long way in making more people aware of your service and can equally earn you good referrals. This way, you also stand the chances of establishing resourceful relationships with potential investors.

Step Five: Leverage your Broker's Marketing Platform

Some forex brokers often promote their top performing PAMM managers based on some specified criteria. You can make efforts and strive to meet the criteria. This way, you can feature on your broker's marketing platform and further publicize your PAMM account offerings. Some brokers also offer referrals to investors. Whichever is the case, endeavor to maximize the opportunities offered by your broker. They can be helpful in attracting investors for your PAMM account.

Step Six: Make your Terms Competitive

You should realize that you have competitors. Hence, you should devise intelligent strategies to have an edge over them. Investors will be attracted to you more than your competitors if you have quality service and still make your terms competitive. You can make your PAMM account structure attractive to investors by charging reasonable management fees, demanding low minimum investment requirements and having flexible withdrawal options. You may also consider offering some sort of incentives and bonus packages to new investors. Also seek means of rewarding long standing investors. These can help you build momentum and also encourage investors.

Step seven: Have a Good Communication Culture

It is important to always maintain good communication with your investors. Ensure to keep your communication with them open and clear. Provide them with regular updates on the performance of your PAMM account. Also, give them information on market conditions, and if you make any changes on your trading strategy, or approach towards risk management, keep them informed.

Some people consider it really difficult to attract investors who would invest in their PAMM account. While the process may not be very smooth and easy, diligently following the steps highlighted in this article can position you on the right track. You need the right information to enable you attract investors. And the right information is what this article offers you.

CHAPTER SEVENTEEN

CAN INVESTOR'S PAMM INVESTMENTS BE MANIPULATED?

Trading has significantly evolved in recent times, offering various avenues for investors to engage and have good returns. PAMM investment is one of such avenues through which investors are able to maximize the opportunities and benefits in trading. This is a popular investment tool that allows investors to pool their capital and invest through experienced traders or money managers. This way, without an in-depth knowledge about trading, individuals can still engage and make returns passively.

While this system offers a gateway for investors to benefit from the financial markets, they also raise significant questions about transparency, risk, and the potential for manipulation.

The main focus of this section is to clarify whether PAMM investments can be manipulated.

HOW PAMM INVESTMENTS WORK

1. Pooling of Funds by Investors: Investors deposit their funds into a single account managed by a trader. For example, if three investors contribute $15,000, $20,000, and $10,000 respectively, the total fund available for trading is $45,000.

2. Trading by the PAMM Manager: The PAMM manager uses his expertise to trade on behalf of the investors. The manager may employ various strategies based on market conditions and their trading style.

3. Profit sharing: Profits or losses are calculated and distributed among the investors according to their respective shares in the total fund. If the account generates a profit of 10%, the return to each would be pro proportional to their investment.

4. Reporting: Most reputable PAMM providers ensure transparency through regular reporting on account performance, which includes details about trades executed and overall returns.

CAN PAMM INVESTMENTS BE MANIPULATED?

Despite its benefits and potentials, this can equally be manipulated. Here are some potential ways manipulation can occur in PAMM investments:

1. Misleading Performance Reporting

It is possible for some PAMM managers to present inflated or misleading performance reports in order to attract investors. For instance, they might cherry-pick favorable periods to showcase high returns, refusing to disclose poor performance during downturns. Some manipulative managers also use false claims to exaggerate their expertise or success rates to lure investors into trusting them with their capital. This selective reporting can mislead potential investors, giving a misrepresentation of the manager's actual capabilities.

2. Fraudulent Activity

In extreme cases, some manipulative managers may engage in outright fraud. This may include falsifying trading records where a manager fabricates trading results to portray a more successful track record than reality. Also by running a ponzi scheme where manipulative managers use new investors' funds to pay returns to earlier investors, creating the illusion of profitability while never generating legitimate profits.

3. High-Risk Strategies

Even without malicious intent, managers may employ excessively high-risk strategies that can lead to significant losses. In some cases, they may engage in aggressive trading to boost short-term performance, which could ultimately harm investors.

4. Conflicts of Interest

PAMM managers often have their own capital invested in the same account they manage. While this alignment of interests can be beneficial, it can also lead to conflicts. For example, a manager may take excessive risks with investor funds to achieve higher returns quickly, prioritizing personal gain over investor safety. Also, if a manager has a significant personal stake in the account's performance, he might withdraw profits before significant drawdowns occur, leaving investors exposed to potential losses.

5. Lack of Regulation

The regulatory environment surrounding PAMM accounts varies significantly by jurisdiction. In many cases, PAMM accounts operate under less stringent regulations compared to other traditional investments like mutual funds. PAMM services that are not subject to strict regulatory scrutiny have high chances of being manipulated by unscrupulous managers. Also, without robust regulatory frameworks in place, investors may find it challenging to seek recourse in cases of fraud or mismanagement.

SAFETY MEASURES AGAINST MANIPULATION

There are several measures that investors can take to protect themselves from potential manipulation in their PAMM investments. This includes the following:

1. Due Diligence

Investors are advised to conduct thorough research before selecting a PAMM manager. Some due diligence checks include the following:

• Review the manager's track record over an extended period rather than relying solely on promotional materials.

• Investigate the manager's qualifications, trading experience, and reputation within the trading community.

• Assess how the manager approaches risk management and whether they have mechanisms in place to mitigate potential losses.

• Choose managers who provide clear and regular reporting on account performance and trading activities.

2. Regulatory Compliance

Investing with brokers that are regulated by reputable authorities can offer an additional layer of security. Brokers that are subject to strict regulations are more likely to enforce compliance measures that protect investor interests.

3. Understanding Fees and Terms
It's essential for investors to understand the fee structure associated with PAMM accounts. Understanding how performance fees are calculated and any potential hidden charges can help avoid unpleasant surprises and manipulations.

4. Monitoring Investments
It is advised for investors to actively monitor their investments. Many PAMM providers offer dashboards with real-time performance data, enabling investors to keep track of their portfolios. Regularly reviewing performance can help detect any concerning trends early.

CHAPTER EIGHTEEN

HOW PROFITABLE IS FOREX MAM INVESTMENT

Understanding various investment strategies is crucial for maximizing returns in the world of finance and investment. The forex MAM investment is one such strategy that has gained attention in recent years. This strategy allows for efficient allocation of resources and potential for higher returns. Forex MAM investment has become popular in forex trading, but the question that still persists is how profitable is this investment technique?

This section will explore the profitability of the forex MAM investment, the factors that influence its profitability, and how to effectively engage with this investment model.

UNDERSTANDING FOREX MAM INVESTMENT

A multi-account management system, or MAM investment, enables a fund manager to oversee several trading accounts at once. This method is particularly popular in the forex market, where skilled traders may manage multiple accounts for distinct clients and place trades using a single interface. Based on each account's equity, the forex MAM system distributes profits and losses proportionately to each one.

FEATURES OF THE FOREX MAM INVESTMENT

Highlighted below are some of the features of the forex MAM investment:

i. Professional Management

The forex MAM system allows investors to benefit from the expertise of seasoned traders who manage their accounts. It is an ideal choice for those who lack the time or knowledge to trade independently.

ii. Flexibility

The MAM system enables flexibility for investors, as it allows for varying investment amounts. This means that clients can choose how much they want to invest without being tied to a minimum threshold.

iii. Transparent Reporting

MAM investment platforms typically provide detailed reports on performance, making it easier for investors to track their returns and understand the strategies employed by the manager.

iv. Risk Management

MAM investment systems often incorporate risk management strategies to help protect investor capital and optimize returns.

Haven considered the features of this unique investment strategy, let us now consider some of the factors that influence its profitability.

FACTORS THAT INFLUENCES THE PROFITABILITY OF THE FOREX MAM INVESTMENT

1. Expertise of the Manager

This is perhaps the most crucial factor that influences the profitability of forex MAM investment. The success of a MAM investment is heavily dependent on the expertise and experience of the fund manager. A successful manager with a proven track record of generating consistent returns is more likely to deliver profitable results. A good MAM manager can be evaluated based on his years of trading experience and also based on a review of his performance history. This will show the manager's ability to navigate various market conditions.

2. Market Conditions

Given the unpredictable nature of the forex market, certain factors such as economic indicators, geopolitical events, and changes in market sentiment can affect profitability. The overall market conditions usually have significant impacts on even forex MAM investment. Volatile market conditions can be more profitable for MAM, when traders capitalize on price swings. However, adverse market conditions can also lead to losses.

3. Trading Strategy

The trading strategy employed by the account manager is crucial to the profitability of the forex MAM investment. Having a well-defined strategy that aligns with the investor's goals can really enhance profitability. Some common trading strategies that are also profitable include the following:

•   **Scalping:** Scalping involves making numerous trades throughout the day to capture small price movements.

•   **Swing Trading:** Swing trading strategy aims to make profit from short term to medium term price movements.

•   **Trend Following:** In this case, managers may employ strategies that seek to capitalize on sustained price movements in one direction.

4. Risk Management

In order to prevent the loss of investor's capital, it is important to adhere to effective risk management practices. The ability of the account manager to manage risk through techniques like stop-loss orders and position sizing can significantly influence profitability. Furthermore, a well-diversified MAM portfolio can help to manage risks and enhance profitability. Diversification across different assets or trading strategies can reduce exposure to any single market event.

5. Trading Platform

Another major factor that can influence the profitability of the forex MAM investment is the trading platform used by the account manager. A good platform should be reliable, efficient, and capable of handling multiple accounts simultaneously. Using a robust platform can greatly enhance trading execution and minimize errors.

At this point, we shall also highlight the pros and cons of this investment strategy.

PROS AND CONS OF FOREX MAM INVESTMENT

The pros of the MAM include the following:

1. Access to professional management is definitely one of the most significant advantages of forex MAM investments. This is particularly beneficial for investors who may lack the time or experience to trade effectively on their own.

2. This strategy allows for diversification across different currency pairs and trading strategies. This further helps in managing the risks associated with market volatility. Investors can better protect their capital from adverse market movements by spreading investments across various assets.

3. Another benefit of forex MAM investments is that it offers scalability by allowing investors to participate with varying account sizes. This implies that different investors can engage without restrictions of minimum deposit requirements. Given the proportional allocation of trades, all accounts can benefit from the manager's strategies, regardless of size.

The following are some of the cons of forex MAM investment:

1. Lack of control is one of the primary drawbacks of MAM investments. Investors utterly rely entirely on the manager's expertise and strategies.

2. Forex MAM accounts usually involve management and performance fees. These fees, though justifiable, can equally eat into the investor's profit.

3. MAM accounts are subject to market risks. Consequently, fluctuations in currency values, geopolitical events, and economic indicators can lead to losses.

CHAPTER NINETEEN

DIFFERENCE BETWEEN PAMM AND MAM ACCOUNTS

The PAMM and MAM accounts are currently two popular account types that cater to different investor needs. While both serve the purpose of allowing investors to benefit from the expertise of professional traders, they operate differently. In this section, we will explore both the PAMM and MAM account types, particularly expounding on the differences between them. This will not only make you more knowledgeable, but will also help you decide which might be best for your investment strategy.

HOW PAMM ACCOUNTS WORK

Structure

In a PAMM setup, multiple investors pool their resources into a single account managed by a trader. Each investor's contribution is represented as a percentage of the total capital in the account.

Profit Sharing

After trading activities conclude, profits (or losses) are distributed among investors based on their initial investment proportions. For instance, if an investor contributed 10% of the total capital, they would receive 10% of the profits.

Manager's Fee

The trader managing the PAMM account typically takes a performance fee, which is deducted before profits are distributed to investors.

Haven understood what PAMM accounts are and how they work, let us now consider MAM accounts.

HOW MAM ACCOUNTS WORK

Individual Accounts

Each investor has their own trading account, but these accounts are managed collectively by a trader. This allows for tailored strategies based on individual risk tolerance and investment goals.

Custom Allocation

Unlike PAMM accounts, where profit distribution is uniform based on percentage ownership, MAM accounts allow for customized allocation of trades across different accounts. This means that one investor might have a different risk exposure than another, even if they are part of the same MAM setup.

Fee Structure

Similar to PAMM accounts, MAM managers charge fees based on performance or management services; however, the fee structure can vary significantly depending on the agreement between the manager and investors.

We have been able to give a quick rundown of both account types. At this point, we are now going to spot some of the major differences between both of them.

KEY DIFFERENCES BETWEEN PAMM AND MAM ACCOUNTS

To better understand the differences between both structures, we will compare them across several dimensions as follows:

1. Management Style

While PAMM accounts entail a single pooled account that is managed by one trader, MAM accounts entail individual accounts that are managed collectively.

2. Profit Distribution

Profit distribution for PAMM accounts is based on percentage of total investment, but for MAM accounts, it is customizable per individual account.

3. Flexibility
PAMM accounts entail limited flexibility as all investors share the same trade. On the other hand, MAM accounts entail higher flexibility, allowing tailored strategies for investors.

4. Investor Control
This is minimal for PAMM accounts as investors have no control over individual trades. MAM accounts on the other hand allows for more control over risk and strategy.

5. Performance Fees
While PAMM accounts apply a fixed performance fee, MAM accounts allow for a more variable performance fee based on agreements.

ADVANTAGES OF PAMM ACCOUNTS
1. PAMM accounts are straightforward for investors who prefer a hands-off approach to trading.
2. Investors can diversify their portfolios by allocating funds to multiple PAMM managers with different trading strategies.
3. Investors benefit from the knowledge and experience of professional traders without needing extensive market knowledge themselves.

DISADVANTAGES OF PAMM ACCOUNTS
1. Investors have no say in trading decisions, relying entirely on the manager's expertise.
2. Managers typically charge high performance fees that can eat into profits.
3. Like all investments, there is a risk of capital loss, especially if the manager underperforms.

ADVANTAGES OF MAM ACCOUNTS
1. Investors retain control over their individual accounts while benefiting from collective management.
2. MAM accounts can be customized according to each investor's preferences and risk tolerance.

3. Investors can monitor their individual performance separately from others in the group.

DISADVANTAGES OF MAM ACCOUNTS

1. The structure can be more complex than PAMM accounts, requiring more understanding from investors.

2. Some MAM setups may require higher minimum investments compared to PAMM accounts.

3. Fees may vary greatly depending on the manager's strategy and success rate.

CHOOSING BETWEEN PAMM AND MAM ACCOUNTS

When choosing between PAMM and MAM accounts, it is essential to consider your investment goals:

• If you prefer a completely hands-off approach with minimal involvement in trading decisions, a PAMM account may be suitable for you.

• If you desire more control over your investments and want tailored strategies that align with your risk tolerance, consider opting for a MAM account.

CONCLUSION

Both PAMM and MAM accounts offer unique advantages and disadvantages, and are tailored to different types of investors in forex trading. Understanding these differences can help you make informed decisions about where to allocate your funds effectively. Ultimately, whether you choose a PAMM or MAM account will depend on your personal investment strategy, risk appetite, and level of desired involvement in trading activities.

CHAPTER TWENTY

PERSONAL TRADING VS. FUND MANAGEMENT

Two common methods of approaching investment management are personal trading and fund management. Each approach offers distinct advantages, potential drawbacks, and levels of involvement suitable to different types of investors. Whether you're an individual with some capital to grow or a high-net-worth individual seeking to invest on a larger scale, understanding the core differences between personal trading and fund management is essential.

In this section, we will break down the key concepts of personal trading and fund management, analyzing their respective strengths and weaknesses. We'll also discuss which option may be more appropriate depending on various investor profiles and financial objectives.

UNDERSTANDING PERSONAL TRADING

Personal trading refers to the practice of individuals making investment decisions for their own capital in the financial markets. These traders have full control over which assets they trade, including stocks, bonds, commodities, and forex, as well as when to enter or exit positions. Personal trading can take many forms, from day trading to swing trading or long-term buy-and-hold investing.

CHARACTERISTICS OF PERSONAL TRADING

1. **Autonomy and Control:** Personal traders make their own decisions without the influence of outside advisors or fund managers. They have the freedom to choose their strategies, risk levels, and portfolio structure.

2. **Learning Opportunity:** Personal trading provides the opportunity for individuals to gain deep knowledge of markets. Traders must develop skills in technical analysis, fundamental analysis, risk management, and understanding market trends.

3. **Access to Various Markets:** Personal traders can trade in various markets such as forex, equities, commodities, and cryptocurrency, giving them a broad spectrum of investment opportunities.

4. **Direct Impact:** The results of personal trading (whether gains or losses) are borne solely by the trader. There are no management fees, which can cut into profits, but at the same time, the trader shoulders all the risks.

PROS OF PERSONAL TRADING

1. **Flexibility:** Traders can enter and exit positions based on their own analysis and convictions, rather than being constrained by institutional guidelines or mandates.

2. **Lower Costs:** There are no fees paid to fund managers or financial advisors. Brokerage fees might apply, but these are typically minimal for retail traders.

3. **Potential for High Returns:** If a trader is skilled, there is the potential for significant profits, especially if they are able to capitalize on market inefficiencies or short-term price movements.

CONS OF PERSONAL TRADING

1. **Time-Consuming:** Successful personal trading requires constant monitoring of the markets, analysis of data, and adaptation to new information. This level of involvement can become a full-time job.

2. **Higher Risk Exposure:** Without professional guidance, personal traders may expose themselves to higher risks. Inadequate risk management strategies or a lack of diversification can lead to significant losses.

3. **Limited Access to Institutional Tools:** While there are many tools available for retail traders, they may lack access to sophisticated trading platforms, research, and liquidity compared to institutional investors.

UNDERSTANDING FUND MANAGEMENT

Fund management refers to the practice of managing a pool of capital from multiple investors, with the goal of generating returns in accordance with the fund's strategy. This could involve hedge funds, mutual funds, pension funds, or exchange-traded funds (ETFs). Fund managers are professionals responsible for the investment decisions, allocation of assets, risk management, and ongoing monitoring of the portfolio's performance.

CHARACTERISTICS OF FUND MANAGEMENT

1. **Professional Expertise:** Fund management is typically executed by experienced financial professionals or firms with a deep understanding of market dynamics, asset allocation, and risk management. These managers use advanced research and tools to make informed investment decisions.

2. **Regulation and Transparency:** Many funds, particularly mutual funds and pension funds are subject to regulatory oversight, providing a level of investor protection that isn't present in personal trading. Regular reporting ensures transparency and accountability to investors.

3. **Access to Large-Scale Opportunities:** Fund managers have access to investments, research, and trading platforms that are often unavailable to individual traders. Institutional buying power can lead to lower transaction costs and better execution.

PROS OF FUND MANAGEMENT

1. **Professional Management:** Investors benefit from the expertise and resources of seasoned fund managers who have access to institutional-grade research, analytics, and tools.

2. **Diversification:** With pooled capital, fund managers can spread risk across various markets, asset classes, and industries, potentially reducing the impact of market volatility on the portfolio.

www.ingramcontent.com/pod-product-compliance
Lightning Source LLC
Chambersburg PA
CBHW070118230526
45472CB00004B/1308

Access to Tools: Personal trading provides limited access to tools unlike fund management that provides access to sophisticated tools.

Time Commitment: Personal trading requires significant time for research and monitoring trades. On the other hand, fund management requires minimal time commitment from investors since they are managed by professionals.

WHICH IS RECOMMENDED AND WHY?

Personal trading is recommended when:
- You Have a High-Risk
- You Seek Full Control
- You Have Time to Devote to Trading
- You Want to Develop Trading Skills

On the other hand, fund management is recommended when:
- You Prefer Passive Investing
- You Want Diversification and Lower Risk
- You Seek Professional Expertise
- You Value Stability and Regulation

CONCLUSION

The choice between personal trading and fund management ultimately depends on your financial goals, risk tolerance, and time commitment. For individuals who enjoy taking an active role in their investments, personal trading can be a fulfilling option. On the other hand, if you prefer a more passive approach, fund management is likely the better option.

By carefully considering your own financial objectives and personal circumstances, you can choose the option that aligns best with your investment philosophy and long-term goals.

3. Passive Investment: For investors who prefer not to be involved in the day-to-day management of their investments, fund management provides a more hands-off approach. Fund managers take care of all the decision-making and adjustments to the portfolio.

CONS OF FUND MANAGEMENT

1. Management Fees: Fund management involves costs such as management fees and, in some cases, performance fees. These fees can eat into the returns, especially if the fund underperforms.

2. Less Control: Investors have little to no control over the specific investment decisions made by the fund manager. They must trust the manager's expertise and strategy, even during periods of underperformance.

3. High Minimum Investment Requirements: Many hedge funds or institutional-grade fund management opportunities come with high minimum investment thresholds, which may exclude smaller individual investors.

PERSONAL TRADING VS. FUND MANAGEMENT: KEY DIFFERENCES

To understand which approach is better suited for you, it's important to break down the key differences between personal trading and fund management.

Control: While personal trading allows full control over investments, fund management allows for minimal control over specific investments.

Risk: Personal trading has potentials for higher risks relative to fund management.

Cost: Personal trading does not require management fees and therefore has lower costs compared to fund management which requires management fees and entails higher cost.